How Money YouTube

MW00875489

The Ultimate Honest Guide for Making Money on YouTube

Table Of Contents

Introduction

I want to thank you for downloading this book, *"How to Make Money Online with YouTube: The Ultimate Honest Guide for Making Money on YouTube."* This book contains proven steps and strategies on how to use the power of YouTube in order to earn income online.

So, you have now delved into the world of online marketing and the infinite possibilities it provides... There are many online offers spreading all over the internet about making quick, easy money without working hard.

Let's start by first accepting that the premise that you can earn large amounts of money online with no hard work is a complete lie. These claims are often coming from marketers or companies that have pipe dreams to sell to naive people who are on hard times. The truth is, the way you make money, whether online or offline, is by providing VALUE to others, at a profit. This value can be in the form of products or services.

Money is given in exchange for the value that is provided.

This may seem obvious to some, but I'm sure a small portion of people reading this book bought it thinking that you can make money with YouTube by spending almost no time upfront and still somehow develop a solid income stream.

Regardless, it is true that there is money to be made out on the internet and anyone can tap into this amazing large reservoir of wealth, but the question is how? This small guide will help you find a unique and fun way of making money online and this is through the ever popular video sharing site, YouTube.

If making videos interests you and you are fond of the creative process, then making money with YouTube is the thing for you. Thanks again for downloading this book and I hope you can pick out some useful nuggets that have worked for me and others that I have talked to and researched!

Be sure to take notes and IMPLEMENT what you are learning in these pages so that you can get the results. The easiest part of your journey will be to read material just like this, the hard part, which will separate you from other video creators, is going to be the actions that you take in order to reach your goals.

Chapter 1:

Getting Started - Creating a Name for Yourself

Before everything else, we must come up with the single most important thing needed to define who you are and what your contribution to YouTube will be - your *username*.

One of the most important things to keep in mind when creating a YouTube channel is coming up with a catchy username. People often make the mistake of rushing through the set-up of their channel and not coming up with a username that can generate buzz. You may have awesome videos, but people on the Internet may not remember you if your username doesn't stand out.

Think about how many videos you've seen online in the last week or even the last few days. Now out of all those videos, think about how many of the channels' usernames you actually remembered. Chances are, you only remember the usernames that were catchy and/or unique. The reason this is so important is because you want everybody who has ever watched one of your videos to be able to search for the channel again, even if it is six months or a year later.

Not everyone on the Internet has a YouTube account so the best way for them to go back to your channel is by searching your username on YouTube. Unless your username is easy to remember, you will have a hard time developing a large audience for your content.

Here are a few things you should take note of when coming up with your own username.

Adding Characters = BIG NO!

You have already thought of using your nickname "Cutie Pie" as your YouTube username. However, when you found out that it was already taken, you got a little frustrated.

Since you are in a rush to create an account, you are just going to add a few "X's" and some numbers to make it look a little more unique. So finally you've come up with "xXxCutiePie143xXx." Yes, you will have a unique name, but such a name will be hard to remember and this is one very big mistake.

Try experimenting on your username without making it hard for other people to recall it. You may include a few words that suit you and/or your channel. "CutieThePie" may look a lot better and sound a little more interesting compared to the one with a lot of "X's" and numbers.

Always Be Readable

Apart from "*xXxCutiePie143xXx*" being difficult to remember, it is also very hard to read from a brief glance. People these days, especially on YouTube, are looking for quick content that satisfies their need at the moment. They aren't looking to remember channel names that are very long.

An important thing to note is that people should be able to easily read and understand your username when they see it. It is also important to stress where the capital letters should be. "TheQuickBrownFox" is more readable than "thequickbrownfox".

Arouse People's Curiosity

Having a catchy username is also important in inviting people to view your videos. A username like "BrownPanda" can catch the attention of some people. Where on earth could they find a brown panda? Try to think about usernames that actually ignite the curiosity of people.

This may draw people to watch what you have to offer even if they had no idea what your videos are actually about. This is especially important if someone were to see your video on the side bar along with other random videos, because they actually have a reason to click if their curiosity is aroused.

Consider Your Topics

You should choose a username that would best describe the videos you are offering. If you are planning on doing videos about cooking, recipes and food, you might opt for "TheYoutubeChef". If you are offering some piano tutorials on YouTube, you can just use "ThePianoTutorialMaster."

These usernames are self-explanatory and they already give your potential viewers an idea of what they are going to see when they visit your channel. People who are also searching for the kinds of videos you are showing can also easily find you.

Another important thing to remember is that you don't want to limit your channel name by making it so specific that you can no longer branch your topics out. For example, if you went with "TheYoutubeChef" and you wanted to start talking about fitness along with your food topics, it would start to get confusing to the viewers who just want your cooking, recipes, and food information.

Don't Rush It

If up until now you haven't really decided on a username yet, take a break. Do not force yourself to create a username just for the sake of making one. Decide on your username carefully because it is something that will define you and your YouTube channel. A great way to come up with a few potential names is to brainstorm all the topics that you want to cover on your channel.

Write them all down on a piece of paper and start to think about words that you can give you credibility to associate with them. For example, if you want to teach about certain topics you can think of words like "Guru" or "Reviewer" to add to the end of your name.

Using Your Own Name

Many people think about using their own name on a YouTube channel. This is definitely an option but it is important to remember that it will be harder to initially gain a lot of viewers if you are using your own name because the people who come across your videos will not have any background info on what you are going to present to them. Just remember that getting that initial traffic to your videos will be more difficult than if you were to use a descriptive username.

Chapter 2:

Content above Everything Else

Of course, having a catchy username is not enough to gain long-term viewers and subscribers on YouTube. Another important thing to consider is the content of your videos. You may have that very inviting username but when your videos do not arouse the interest of your viewers once they get there, your efforts will have gone to waste. Or when you have a username "PianoTutorials" but very few of your videos even show piano tutorials, viewers will get disappointed and will just leave.

Your videos are actually what gives life to your YouTube channel. A channel that has no relevant or interesting videos is of no use to anyone. Bear in mind that people who visit

YouTube are there because they are looking for videos that have interesting content. They have many options at their disposal so if you aren't interesting enough to hold their attention, the chances are that they will go looking for another channel to watch.

Maintain a category for your channel

Some channels gain their subscribers because they stick to a certain category. Think of a channel which offers videos featuring animals. A lot of animal lovers would subscribe to this channel. A YouTube channel dedicated to posting official movie trailers is followed by some users because that's what they expect to see from this channel. Now think of a channel that posts nothing but random irrelevant content. You will never know what to expect to see on the next video.

You probably would not choose to subscribe to that channel at all because the reason people subscribe to channels is rarely because of the past videos that are on there. Almost all people that subscribe to a YouTube channel do it because they are expecting more of what they've already seen.

One way to keep viewers is to maintain a certain category. If your channel is merely for entertainment, then your viewers will expect your videos to be entertaining. If your channel is for comic relief, then make sure your videos are humorous. Eventually, users who are interested in the kind of videos you make will subscribe to you if you stay consistent.

You may notice that on many of the top YouTube channels, they stick to what works for their channel. Even the biggest channels do not try to upload videos about random topics because they know that the large following that they've built is there for a specific reason.

Provide descriptions for your videos

It is also helpful to provide a description for each of your videos. Do not think all people ignore the description box; a lot really do read what is written there. However, do not provide a full detailed description that could actually spoil the video for some. Instead, write something that insightfully tells the viewers what the video will be about so that they will have an idea of what is coming.

Also, it is important to put disclaimers on the bottom of your description. Maybe you've made a controversial video and you don't want to offend a specific person, or group of people, that could take it the wrong way. This is the place to mention that information so that you don't have to change the content of the video itself too much.

Make your videos interesting

Some videos are so long that viewers actually get tired of watching them, unless, of course, the video is interesting. Your videos should be interesting enough so that viewers would actually watch them until the end. It is not just enough that you gain an audience by very short clips, eventually your viewers will want videos that contain some substance.

The optimal length of videos will always be debated and YouTube has preferred different lengths at different times over the years. However, a strong rule of thumb to go by is to try and keep your videos between 3 to 7 minutes. Keeping your videos close to that 3-minute mark would be great but the problem a lot of YouTube channels run into is that if they make a 3-minute video, it is hard to get enough good content in order to make it worthwhile.

By making your videos longer than 7 minutes, you are risking losing the viewers who were initially interested. It is important to keep in mind that most YouTube viewers are looking for shorter videos because they either want quick information on a topic or want to be entertained. They aren't looking for a long lecture that will take a chunk of time out of their day.

The exception to this is if you are recording podcasts or videos that are meant to be deeply informative to the viewer. Maybe you are going in-depth about an illness or a mental issue and someone may need a strong breakdown of the problem. If you were doing these types of videos, making a short, 3-4 minute video would actually be a let-down for the viewer instead of the in-depth guide that they were looking for. However, if you are providing that much in-depth knowledge, YouTube probably isn't the best medium for you anyways.

Keep your word

If you mentioned in one of your video descriptions that you are going to upload a specific video by a specific date, do upload a video by that date. Your subscribers are actually expecting the video since you have given your word on it. If you fail to do so, humbly apologize to your subscribers in the very next video that you publish. Otherwise, you will lose credibility and it will be very difficult to gain that back.

YouTube viewers are not known for being extremely loyal to channels that are new and just starting off, especially because of the amount of options they have just one click away. Your best bet is to keep your subscribers informed of the new videos coming out and then over-deliver by giving them a little extra content than they originally expected, or maybe even uploading it a day earlier than they had planned for.

It is important to remember that when your channel is in its beginning stages, your best bet is to upload as frequently as possible without sacrificing quality. If you can upload a high number of quality videos in your beginning stage, it will greatly increase your chance of being promoted by YouTube on the side bars of other channel's videos.

The key here is to never sacrifice quality for quantity. If you find yourself pushing to make a video just for the sake of getting it out there, eventually your viewers are going to catch on and realize that you aren't putting in very much effort into your production quality.

Chapter 3:

What Do You Need?

Having a YouTube channel and making sure it delivers interesting videos is not as simple as it may seem. You also have to take note of a few necessities you need in order to run a great channel on YouTube.

Strong Internet connection

This is the one of the most obvious things you should have in order to create a YouTube account. Remember that YouTube is a video-sharing website and that websites are accessed via the internet. To put it simply, you cannot open the YouTube website if you have no Internet connection and uploading videos onto your own channel is a time-consuming process that needs a solid Internet connection.

However, it is not just enough to have an Internet connection. It is also important that your connection is strong and stable. Can you imagine having to re-upload the whole video if your Internet signal suddenly disconnected, even if 99.99% of your video has already been processed. Your videos will get uploaded much later than scheduled, and this would surely affect the credibility of your channel.

It is always best to get a stronger Internet connection than you think you need if you want to commit to pleasing your subscribers. Don't be afraid to spend money on the Internet in your apartment/house if you plan on really developing a solid YouTube channel. This is never something you want to sacrifice and there is no other way around it!

Invest in a quality camera and microphone

Nowadays, people look for videos with high quality. If you give them a video that is too blurry or pixilated, they will not bother to watch for long. Webcams are not the kind of cameras you would want to have your video recorded on, as the video quality they provide isn't as clear as most people desire.

In the last 2-3 years, the quality of videos and pictures on the Internet has really elevated because of the affordability of cameras. Because of this big jump to more quality videos, it is hard for a viewer to take a video seriously if they notice that the video is blurry or lagging when something moves.

It does not necessarily have to be that latest model of a specific camera brand. The important thing to consider is that your camera should be able to capture and produce good quality video as well as audio.

The latest cameras are always being upgraded so don't stress too much on having to own the nicest equipment. You can always upgrade later when you have made some money from your channel and your subscriber base has grown. For now, just get something that can get the job done and allow you to record quality videos.

Who would want to watch to a video with bad visuals and audio? Put yourself in the shoes of the viewer.

Good topics and ideas

You can never have too many possible video ideas. This is extremely important to remember when it comes to the growth of your channel. After you get in the habit of uploading videos on a regular schedule and your subscriber base is growing, the worst thing that can happen is that you run out of ideas and topics to talk about. Unfortunately, it is common to see a mid to large sized YouTube channel almost come to a halt or maybe upload half as much as before once they've maxed out on ideas.

Ideas may come from anywhere: your life, experiences, your neighbor, your work, and your hobbies, among others. It is important for anyone to have a good stream of ideas in order for them to tap the YouTube goldmine. If ideas seem too hard to come by, you can ask your subscribers for some. Leave comments on your videos or create a video asking them to provide ideas. This interaction with your viewers is a great way to create a following. Finally, the internet is the largest place where ideas are stored. A simple 1 to 2 hours of surfing the net may give you the spark you need to whip up a successful video.

Remember that a video with high-quality visuals and audio will be useless if it does not contain accurate, fresh, and interesting content.

Target audience

Another thing you need to consider for your YouTube channel is the people who will benefit the most from your videos, also known as your target audience. You must make sure that you have potential viewers. It is just like starting a new business. You must have potential customers in mind before you start the business because if you decide who the customers are after the business is up and running, you risk a high chance of failure.

Finding a target audience is also important because it will greatly help your chance of marketing and growing your channel as time goes on. You will know what online forums to promote your channel on, you can network and collaborate with other YouTube channels, as well as understand the problems and/or questions your audience will have.

Having a target audience will also help you to know what stance to take on certain issues that you will come across in the future. Because you are on YouTube, you will be susceptible to criticism from all types of people and by having a strong support system from your target audience, you will get a better understanding of what criticisms you can actually use to help further your channel. Most negative feedback you receive will not be able to help you if your videos have no target audience because you can't pinpoint where the feedback is coming from. However, you can actually take some advice from your viewers if you understand their

background, their intentions, and can relate to
them.

Chapter 4:

All About YouTube

YouTube is a website created by three former PayPal employees in February of 2005 and is now owned by Google. It is a video sharing site that attracts millions of people worldwide. This is one of the major gold mines on the Internet and it is a great opportunity for people trying to share ideas and information by entertaining at the same time.

YouTube for video sharing

Registered users are able to upload their videos and have the public see those videos for free. The wide range of videos you can find on YouTube include documentaries, short films, musical performances, vlogs, how-to instructionals, and even educational shows. Some of these are uploaded by individuals and others by large organizations. This is why videos can include both amateur and professional production, depending on who the publisher is.

Pretty much any form of expression can be uploaded onto YouTube. The instances where YouTube may terminate your account is if you do not follow their terms or if your videos contain pornography, obscenity, or forms of copyright infringement.

Connecting with the YouTube community

YouTube also allows you to subscribe to interesting channels so that you can refer back to them in the future. This way, it will be easier for you to follow and keep track of certain kinds of videos that you like. The ability to rate and comment on videos allows you to connect and share your ideas and opinions with the rest of the YouTube community.

YouTube to express yourself

Let's say you are an aspiring singer. You may actually post a video of yourself singing. A number of people have actually been discovered by major record labels and eventually became famous, all because they took the risk of showing their talents to the world, with the risk of criticism. Justin Bieber and Greyson Chance are two notable examples.

YouTube Partnership Program

Unbeknownst to many, YouTube also offers a partnership program that can help you improve your skills, build your audience and monetize your videos. You have to meet the following criteria so that YouTube can consider you to be part of the YouTube partnership program:

The program is available in your country. (If not available, you may need to apply through an application form.)

Your account is in good standing and has not been disabled for monetization.

Content that you upload must be original and advertiser-friendly.

Your video content complies with YouTube's Terms of Service and Community Guidelines.

You have properly reviewed YouTube's copyright education materials.

Note that you cannot monetize videos which contain material created by another person without his or her explicit permission.

Here are the steps on how to check if your channel is eligible to avail the program:

Go to the Monetization tab in your account settings.

If your account is in good standing and has not been previously disabled for monetization, click "Enable My Account."

Follow the steps to accept the YouTube Monetization agreement.

A different message may appear if your account is not enabled for monetization.

Take note that monetizing your content means that selected advertisements will be displayed on your video. In order to earn money from these advertisements, you must first associate an AdSense account with your account on YouTube. You will receive your payment once you monetize one of your videos and once you reach your local AdSense payment threshold. These thresholds vary depending on the currency of your AdSense account.

For the most part, the number of views your video gets determines the amount of money you will make. On average, advertisers on YouTube pay out around $1 for every 1,000 views. With a ratio of $1 for every 1,000 views, having a million views would guarantee you earnings of close to $1,000.

It is important to note that YouTube also offers special services to the members of their partnership program. These special services are to incentivize people to work hard at building their channels to a certain level where YouTube feels comfortable helping them to earn even more income with more opportunities.

In turn, YouTube earns more money as a company because the channels that are working hard to create quality content are bringing money back into YouTube's pockets.

Many YouTube channels complain about some of the limitations that YouTube places on their account. However, keep in mind that the reason YouTube is able to enforce such strong rules and guidelines on their videos, is because they are by far the most popular video sharing site in the world. This means that if you were try to become a successful video content producer outside of YouTube it would be extremely difficult.

Chapter 5:

Promoting Yourself

You already have your YouTube channel up and have some interesting videos to share to the public. But wait! How will you let other people know about you, let alone get them to watch your videos? Here are some ways you can promote your channel.

Other social media sites

Posting your YouTube video links to other social media sites will help you reach a wider audience.

There are a lot of people who are more active on other social networks, such as Facebook and Twitter, and wouldn't have come across your content otherwise. Sharing your YouTube videos through those other social networks will invite users even from outside YouTube. As you probably know by now, you don't necessarily have to sign up with YouTube just to watch the videos featured there.

If you have put up a new video, share the link and give a brief description to the relevant communities on other social media sites. At first you may feel uncomfortable with posting these videos up, however, remember that if you honestly feel like you've put hard work into these videos, there is no reason why you can't share it with others. If you are on these forums, be sure to contribute often and do not only post something when you are self-promoting. This will come off as "spammy" and people will become turned off. Focus on providing value first, then promoting yourself.

Share with friends

You can start by sharing your videos with your friends. If your videos are interesting enough, your friends may share your videos with their friends. Before you know it, you have built a small grassroots audience that is willing to give you great feedback before you are getting a lot of traffic.

Video response

Another way to promote yourself on YouTube is to make video responses to videos posted by other users. Create an interesting and relevant video response to a video that you like. Chances are that the viewers of that video will also watch your video response.

If you decide to make a video response, be sure not to attack anybody who is publishing his or her own videos. It is perfectly fine to comment on the ideas that a person has, or the content of their video, but stay away from attacking the person themselves. Trying to attack a large channel can ruin your YouTube career, as you will be flooded with people disliking your videos and this is not easy to overcome at the very beginning.

Narrow down user's search

YouTube has videos about pretty much every single topic you can think of. If you want to post a video of a dog, you would not want to have a title as "Dog" only, right? When users search for "dog" in YouTube, there would be a ton of results that would come up. However, take note that users normally search for a video with a dog doing something specific, for example, they may search for "dog tricks". They would actually narrow down their search by using the keywords "dog tricks." Your video will not automatically show up among all the other results even if it features dog tricks, unless you have the phrase in your title.

Write as many descriptive keywords for your video as you can in the "tags" section of your video description. This will help users more easily find your video when they do their search.

Be active in the YouTube community

Since YouTube is another social community on the internet, it is better if you interact with the rest of the YouTube users out there. When you see a video you like, do not hesitate to give it a good rating. You know how hard it is to make a video that would interest your users. If feels great to receive feedback from your viewers so do the same thing for the videos that you are watching. Other YouTubers will really appreciate it and they will often return the favor.

Participate in YouTube contests that are held by other users. Submit your own entry so that viewers who are following the contest will be likely to check your channel out.

Be active in other related forums and websites

A great way to get instant exposure to your channel is to be involved on other platforms that discuss the topics you present in your videos. For example, if you have a channel regarding painting, you can go to a forum on a website about painting and mention how you think you can help the readers out. This is a great way to make a strong impact and develop a loyal following.

The reason this is so beneficial is because you already know that the people on these sites are interested in the same topics you are making your videos on. Make sure to be active on these sites as well, so you can possibly network with others. They may also be more willing to share your videos with others if they find your interactions to be pleasant.

The DO-NOT-DO's

There are also a few things you need to take note of when promoting your YouTube channel.

Do not spam. People will find it annoying if you keep sending them your video links without asking about them and providing insightful comments on their content. If they really like your videos, they will return back to your channel even without you encouraging them to do so.

Do not beg for people to watch your videos. Do not force them to subscribe. Again, if your videos are interesting enough for the viewers, they will watch and subscribe to your channel on their own, after you've mentioned it a couple of times. Focus on creating quality content on a consistent basis and your subscribers and views will come with some marketing and exposure. Quality content will get you way more views and more importantly, subscribers, than begging people to watch your videos.

Chapter 6:

Making Money at Last!

You have already set up your YouTube channel, you have already uploaded interesting videos, and you already have a number of viewers as well. You are now thinking of using your YouTube videos to actually earn money. You can monetize your videos by availing to the **YouTube Partnership Program**.

But first, you should make sure you have met the following criteria:

Your video must contain original content. By original, this means you must own all the necessary rights to use material, audio and visuals commercially. DO NOT market videos made by other people as if these were made by you.

The content of your video must be advertiser-friendly.

You understand and agree to YouTube's terms of service and community guidelines.

Take note also that if you have previously applied for monetization and got disapproved, you need to wait for two months before applying again. If the program is not available in your country, you may have to apply through an application form.

If you think your videos can now help you earn money, here is what you do:

Apply for the YouTube partnership program.

Wait for your application to be approved. You need to be patient because this might take up to two weeks.

Once your application is approved, you can now start monetizing all your videos that have met the criteria for eligibility.

Review the YouTube Partnership Program tutorial. Make sure you have not violated any of the rules.

Create a Google AdSense account and link it with your account on YouTube.

Turn on advertisements on your videos.

Keep creating valuable videos and the money will come!

Remember that your number of views is the most important thing that will determine the amount of money you receive. Make sure you keep your viewers coming to increase revenue. The reason subscribers are so important is because when you have subscribers, you are basically guaranteed a certain number of views each time you upload a video. These subscribers are also more likely to share your content because they feel more connected to you then someone who just stumbles across your videos or visits from time to time.

Other ways to earn money

There are also a few other ways of making money through YouTube. After building your channel up to over 50+ videos and a strong subscriber base, you can begin to implement these other techniques to earn even more money from your work.

Advertise a brand

This involves giving endorsements to a certain brand or simply using them on your video. Take for instance, some T-shirt printing business. You could advertise their products by simply wearing a sample shirt while recording a video. This would help them promote their brand and you would actually earn some money that they will pay you directly.

Sell your products

You may actually not just find viewers in the community but also potential customers for your products, if you have any. Your video may not necessarily have to talk about you selling some of your stuff. Just like in the previous example, you may just use it in your video and maybe just add in the description that the certain item is actually for sale. Or you could also choose to be more straightforward and just create a video of you telling your viewers you have something for sale.

Maintain your audience

Your YouTube career has just started. Do not stop just because you already have one of your videos making money for you. It took time for today's successful YouTube stars to get to where they are now. Be patient and persistent. Continue making videos for your subscribers. Keep an upload schedule so your viewers will know when you are going to be releasing a new video. You will find that as your subscriber base grows, you will actually be looking forward to providing new videos, as it becomes something they look forward to. It could be a Wednesday morning ritual to watch your video before they start their day, for example.

Conclusion

Thank you again for downloading this book! This book was an overview of all the strategies used by myself, a few other people that I know personally, as well as others that I have researched. Our channels are all at least two years old and hopefully this book was able to save you some time from all the experimenting that we had to do.

The next step is to apply what you have learned by setting up a YouTube channel, coming up with fresh, relevant, and original content, and using all possible means of increase your number of viewers and subscribers. Remember to be consistent and persistent for your efforts to truly pay off.

Finally, if you enjoyed this book, please take the time to share your thoughts by sending me a personal message. It'd be greatly appreciated and I look forward to hearing from you!

Thank you and good luck on your journey!

Made in the USA
Monee, IL
26 September 2023

43485862R00036